MY INDIAN
KITCHEN

My Indian
KITCHEN

BELINDA NAGY

NEW HOLLAND

Published in 2015 by
New Holland Publishers
London • Sydney • Auckland

The Chandlery Unit 9 50 Westminster Bridge Road London SE1 7QY United Kingdom
1/66 Gibbes Street Chatswood NSW 2067 Australia
5/39 Woodside Ave Northcote, Auckland 0627 New Zealand

www.newhollandpublishers.com

A catalogue record of this book is available at the British Library and the National Library
of Australia.

ISBN: 9781742577029

Managing Director: Fiona Schultz
Project Editor: Holly Willsher
Design: Andrew Quinlan
Production Director: Olga Dementiev
Printer: Toppan Leefung Printing Ltd (China)

10 9 8 7 6 5 4 3 2 1

Follow New Holland Publishers on
Facebook: www.facebook.com/NewHollandPublishers

Contents

Introduction

Indian cuisine is often categorized into four food regions. A more refined breakdown reveals that there are eight distinct areas, all with unique food histories and divergent tastes. Knowledge of each of the regions of India will help you understand the vast array of food in this vibrant cuisine.

North India

The hearty food of the north has Muslim and Moghul influences, resulting in a variety of savoury, rich lamb and goat dishes based on cooking with ghee and cream. The cuisine is further enhanced by the tandoor method of cooking, which was indigenous to the north-west frontier, now the Punjab and Pakistan. The tandoor (clay oven), which burns wood or charcoal, imparts an unparalleled smoky flavour to mildly spiced, tender meats and poultry, fish and breads. Punjabi food is simple and filling, an amalgamation of the cuisines of the Greeks, Persians, Afghans, Moghuls and northern invaders.

Maharashtra

The people of Maharashtra, of which Mumbai is the capital, prepare healthy food with an emphasis on rice, vegetables (as Maharashtrians are generally vegetarians), nuts and nut oils. Often vegetables are spiced with a combination of ground and roasted cumin seeds, sesame seeds, cardamom, cinnamon and coconut. Sweet and sour dishes make for tantalising eating.

Gujarat

From Maharashtra's neighbouring state of Gujarat comes an interesting vegetarian cuisine called thali. The food is oil-free and thali restaurant waiters will refill your bowls until you are full. Thali has become an institution in India's major cities. Gujarati are fond of relishes and pickles.

Sindh

The Sindhis migrated to India after the 1947 partition, bringing with them a cuisine characterised by garlic, mint-flavoured chutneys, pickles and very sweet meats. Sindhi food is not necessarily vegetarian. An example is kofta tas-me. These are meatballs served in a sauce of onion, tomato, chilli, ginger and coriander (cilantro), and sprinkled with garam masala.

Parsi

Like Christians, the Parsis have no religious dietary restrictions. Their cuisine is not overly hot, so it is a favourite with many foreigners. Traditionally, on Sunday, Parsis (most of whom live in Mumbai) add several dhals to meat and chicken and serve them with caramelised brown rice.

Bengal

Freshwater and saltwater fish, seafood and the flavour of mustard seed dominate the Bengali diet. Fish is grilled (broiled), fried or stewed. Yoghurt is offered separately and is sometimes also used in cooking. Bengalis like lightly fried fish in a sauce Westerners would regard as curry-flavoured, yet it is relatively mild. Bengalis also love sweet dishes.

South India

In the south of India one finds a Brahmin cuisine, which is distinct because strict South Indian Brahmins will not eat tomatoes, beetroot, garlic or onions. Recipes are based on tamarind, chilli, coconut, yellow lentils and rice. These, combined with a vegetable, make sambar, a staple dish eaten with rasam, a peppery, lentil-based consommé. These two dishes are the basis of the English-inspired mulligatawny. Meat and seafood are enjoyed by non-vegetarians. Steamed dumplings and pancakes made from fermented ground rice and dhal have spread from Southern India throughout India.

Goa

The Christian Portuguese had a great deal of influence on the tropical state of Goa, as did the Muslims. The Portuguese use of vinegar and the sour candied fruits of lokum and tamarind have combined with the Christian preference for pork and a non-vegetarian Hindu taste for lamb. Seafood, fish and fruits are plentiful. Goans also perfected the vindaloo.

Vegetable samosas

Preheat the oven to 200°C/400°F. Roll pastry out very thin. Cut five 10 cm/4 in-diameter circles from each sheet of pastry. Cut circles in half.

Heat 1 tablespoon of oil in a frying pan and sauté onion for 5 minutes or until clear. Add curry powder and cook for 30 seconds or until curry smells fragrant. Mix potato, peas, onion mixture, parsley and lemon juice together.

Place a teaspoon of potato mixture on each pastry semi-circle. Wet pastry edges and fold dough over to form a cone shape. Cover with a damp kitchen towel while preparing remaining samosas.

Place on a baking sheet and bake for 15 minutes, turning after 10 minutes. Brush with remaining oil and serve immediately.

MAKES 40

4 sheets unsweetened short pastry
3 tbsp peanut oil
1 small onion, finely chopped
1 tsp curry powder
400 g (14 oz) can potatoes, drained
  and quartered
25 g (1 oz) frozen peas
¼ bunch parsley, chopped
1 tbsp lemon juice

Entrées

Chicken Samosas

MAKES 30

250 g (9 oz) chicken mince

350 ml (12 fl oz) vegetable oil

2 medium onions, finely chopped

1 clove garlic, crushed

2 tsp curry paste

½ tsp salt

1 tbsp white vinegar

120 ml (4 fl oz) water

2 tsp sweet chilli sauce

10 g (½ oz) coriander/cilantro, chopped

1 packet frozen spring roll wrappers

Remove the chicken from the refrigerator and bring to room temperature. Heat a wok, add a little oil and fry onions and garlic until soft. Add curry paste and salt and fry a little. Stir in the vinegar. Add chicken mince and stir-fry over high heat until it starts to turn white. Break up any lumps. Reduce heat, add the water, cover and cook until most of the water is absorbed, about 6 minutes. Uncover, add chilli sauce and coriander. Stir until the water has evaporated and mince is dry. Remove to a plate to cool. Rinse wok.

Cut 10 spring roll wrappers into 3 even pieces. Place a teaspoon of filling at bottom end and fold over the pastry diagonally, forming a triangle. Fold again on the straight and continue to fold in same manner. Moisten the inside edge of the last fold with water and press gently to seal. Repeat with remaining wrappers.

Heat the wok and add oil until approximately 5 cm (2 in) deep. Heat oil but take care not to overheat. Add 3 or 4 samosas and fry until golden. Remove with a slotted spoon to a tray lined with absorbent paper. Repeat with remainder. If samosas become too dark, immediately remove from heat to drop the oil temperature.

Vindaloo chicken nuggets

Cut each thigh fillet into 4 pieces. Place in a bowl, sprinkle lightly with salt and pepper then pour over the lemon juice. Toss with spoon to mix through. Rub the vindaloo curry paste well into each piece with your fingers. Cover and refrigerate for 2 hours or more.

Preheat oven to 200°C/390°F. Coat the chicken pieces in flour, dip in the egg, then cover in breadcrumbs. Lightly spray a large flat tray with canola oil spray and add the nuggets. Lightly spray the surface of the nuggets. Bake for 15–18 minutes.

To make the dipping sauce, place the grated cucumber in a strainer and allow to stand a few minutes to drain off excess liquid. Mix into the yoghurt with seasoning and lemon juice.

Serve hot nuggets with yoghurt and cucumber sauce.

MAKES ABOUT 32

1 kg (2 lbs) chicken thigh fillets

salt and pepper

1 tbsp lemon juice

2 tbsp vindaloo curry paste

150 g (5 oz) all-purpose/plain flour

2 eggs, lightly beaten

175 g (6 oz) dried breadcrumbs

canola oil spray

Yoghurt and cucumber dipping sauce

1 Lebanese cucumber, grated

240 ml (8 fl oz) plain yoghurt

salt and pepper

1 tbsp lemon juice

Entrées

Chicken and almond triangles

MAKES 21

500 g (1 lb) chicken mince

1 tbsp olive oil

75 g (3 oz) slivered almonds

1 medium onion, finely chopped

½ tsp salt

1 tsp ground cinnamon

1 tsp paprika

2 tsp ground cummin

2 small tomatoes, chopped

40 g (1½ oz) raisins, chopped

10 g (½ oz) flat-leaf parsley, finely
   chopped

60 ml (2 fl oz) dry white wine

1 packet filo pastry

canola oil spray

Remove chicken from the refrigerator and bring to room temperature. Heat oil in a frying pan and sauté the almonds until pale gold. Quickly remove with a slotted spoon and drain on paper towel. Add onion and fry until soft, stir in salt and spices and cook until aromatic. Add chicken mince and stir-fry until almost cooked. Add tomatoes, raisins, parsley, almonds and wine and simmer, covered, for 15 minutes. Uncover and cook until juices are absorbed. Allow to cool.

Thaw the pastry. Count out 14 sheets, refreeze remainder. Cut into three even strips. Stack and cover with a clean tea towel.

Preheat oven to 180°C/360°F. Take 1 strip, spray one side lightly with canola oil, then put another strip on top, and spray again. Fold in half down the middle, making a long, thin strip. Spray once more. Place a teaspoon of filling on bottom end of each strip. Fold right-hand corner over to form a triangle then fold on the straight, then on the diagonal, repeating until end is reached. Repeat with remaining.

Place triangles on a tray sprayed with oil. Spray tops of triangles with oil and bake for 20–25 minutes. Serve hot as finger food.

Curried chicken rolls

Remove chicken from the refrigerator and bring to room temperature. Heat oil in a small pan, add onion and garlic and fry until onion is soft. Stir in curry paste and cook a little. Add lemon juice and stir to mix. Set aside. Combine the mince, breadcrumbs, salt, pepper and coriander with the onion mixture. Mix well.

Place a thawed sheet of puff pastry on the bench and cut in half across the centre. Take one of these halves and pile a quarter of the mince mixture in a 1 cm (½ in) wide strip along the centre. Brush the exposed pastry at the back with water, lift the front strip of pastry over the filling and roll up. Press lightly to seal. Cut the roll into 4 equal portions. Repeat with second half and then with second sheet. Glaze with milk and sprinkle with sesame seeds. Place on a flat baking tray.

Preheat the oven to 190°C/375°F. Cook for 10 minutes, reduce heat to 180°C/360°F and continue cooking for 15 minutes until golden brown.
Serve hot as finger food.

MAKES 16

500 g (1 lb) chicken mince

2 tsp canola oil

1 medium onion, finely chopped

1 small clove garlic, crushed

2 tsp mild curry paste

1½ tbsp lemon juice

3 tbsp dried breadcrumbs

½ tsp salt

½ tsp pepper

10 g (½ oz) fresh coriander (cilantro) chopped

2 sheets frozen puff pastry

1 tbsp milk

1 tbsp sesame seeds

Entrées

Tandoori chicken pockets

SERVES 4

400 g (14 oz) chicken strips

½ tsp salt

2 tsp canola oil

1 small onion, finely chopped

2 tsp tandoori curry paste

1 tbsp lemon juice

1 tbsp water

8 pieces pita bread

350 g (12 oz) shredded lettuce

120 ml (4 fl oz) natural yoghurt

Cut chicken into small pieces, sprinkle with salt and set aside. Heat the oil in a small pan, add onion and fry until soft. Add the chicken and fry until almost cooked. Stir in the curry paste, cook a little, then add the lemon juice and water. Allow to simmer until most of the liquid has evaporated. Stir occasionally.

Cut the pita bread in half and open the pocket. Place lettuce in the base of the pocket and fill with the curried chicken. Add a tablespoon of yoghurt on top. Serve immediately.

Entrées

Moong sprouts

In a large bowl, mix together the moong sprouts, the onion, salt, turmeric, green masala, ginger, garlic and coriander-cumin.

To make the vagaar, heat the oil in a small pan with a well-fitting lid. Brown the chilli, followed by the cumin seeds. Add the sprout mixture to the pan with the warm water. Cover the pot and cook over a medium heat for about 45 minutes. (The sprouts should be soft but not stick together.) Garnish with the coriander leaves.

Time: 1 hour, 1–2 days for sprouting.

SERVES 4

250 ml (8 fl oz) moong sprouts,
  5 mm (¼ in) long

1 large onion, chopped

1 tsp salt

½ tsp turmeric

1 tsp green masala

½ tsp fresh ginger, pounded

½ tsp fresh garlic, pounded

2 tsp coriander-cumin

VAGAAR

120 ml (4 fl oz) cooking oil

1 dried red chilli

1 tsp cumin seeds

GARNISH

1 tbsp coriander leaves (cilantro),
  chopped

Entrées

Piri Piri-spiced shrimp

SERVES 4

1 kg (2 lbs) medium raw shrimp
  (prawns)
1 tbsp peanut oil
2 tbsp lemon juice
2 tsp piri piri seasoning
2 tsp parsley flakes
1 clove garlic, freshly crushed
50 g (2 oz) plain (all-purpose) flour
vegetable oil for deep-frying

Remove the heads and shells from the shrimps, leaving the tails intact. Using a sharp knife, make an incision along the back of the shrimp, remove the vein and cut into the shrimp so it opens out.

Combine the peanut oil, lemon juice, piri piri seasoning, parsley and garlic in a bowl. Add the shrimps and coat in the mixture. Dip the shrimps lightly in the flour.

Heat the oil in a wok or frying pan. Cook the shrimps in batches for 1–2 minutes or until golden and crisp.

Serve the shrimps with lime wedges.

Soups

Indian-spiced potato and onion soup

SERVES 4

1 tbsp vegetable oil

1 onion, finely chopped

1 cm (½ in) piece root ginger,
*   finely chopped*

2 large potatoes, cut into 1 cm
*   (½ in) cubes*

2 tsp ground cumin

2 tsp ground coriander

½ tsp turmeric

1 tsp ground cinnamon

1 L (1¾ pt) vegetable stock

salt and black pepper

1 tbsp natural yoghurt to
*   garnish*

Heat the oil in a large saucepan. Fry the onion and ginger for 5 minutes or until softened. Add the potatoes and fry for another minute, stirring often.

Mix the cumin, coriander, turmeric and cinnamon with 2 tablespoons of cold water to make a paste. Add to the onion and potato, stirring well, and fry for 1 minute.

Add the stock and season to taste. Bring to the boil, then reduce the heat, cover and simmer for 30 minutes or until the potato is tender. Blend until smooth in a food processor or press through a metal sieve. Return to the pan and gently heat through. Garnish with the yoghurt and more black pepper.

Chilled Yoghurt Soup

Peel and grate the cucumber.

Combine the cream, yoghurt and vinegars together, and whisk lightly, until smooth. Stir in the cucumber, mint, garlic and seasoning. Cover and refrigerate for three hours.

Stir and taste for seasoning before serving chilled. Garnish with a slice of cucumber, a sprig of mint and cracked pepper.

SERVES 4-6

1 large telegraph cucumber
240 ml (8 fl oz) thickened cream
200 ml (7 fl oz) natural yoghurt
2 tbsp white wine vinegar
1 tbsp balsamic vinegar
2 tbsp fresh mint,
chopped
1 clove garlic, crushed
salt and freshly ground
*   black pepper*
extra mint and slices of cucumber,
*   to garnish*

Soups

Smoky lamb & eggplant soup

SERVES 6-8

1 kg (2 lbs) eggplant (aubergines)

85 g (3 oz) ghee or butter

2 large leeks

500 g (1 lb) sweet potato, peeled and cubed

2 tsp ground cumin

2 tsp ground cinnamon

2 kg (4½ lb) lamb shanks

1 L (1¾ pt) beef stock

4 sprigs thyme

3 cinnamon sticks

40 g (1½ oz) flat-leaf parsley, chopped

Prick the eggplants all over and place them on a grill or barbecue, turning often until charred and deflated. Alternatively, bake at 220°C/425°F for 1 hour until the eggplants are soft and deflated. Chop the eggplant, discarding any very tough or charred skin.

Heat half the ghee or butter in a large pan, add the leeks and sauté until golden. Add the chopped eggplant, sweet potato, cumin and ground cinnamon and stir thoroughly while cooking for 5 minutes or until all the ingredients are golden and fragrant. Place this mixture in a bowl and set aside.

In the used pan, heat the remaining ghee or butter and add the lamb shanks, cooking them over a medium-high heat until they are golden all over. Add the beef stock, thyme, cinnamon sticks and 1.5 litres (2½ pints) water and simmer for 1 hour.

Remove the shanks and, to the remaining soup, add eggplant mixture and half the parsley. Simmer for 10 minutes. Meanwhile, cut all meat off the lamb shanks and return this meat to the soup. Discard the bones.

Remove the cinnamon sticks and thyme sprigs, then reheat the soup. Season to taste. Stir well then serve with the remaining parsley and black pepper.

Indian lentil soup

In a large pan, heat ghee and add lentils, mustard seeds, ground coriander, cumin, turmeric, cinnamon, garlic, ginger, curry leaves, onion and green chilli. Cook over low heat for 5 minutes until spices are aromatic and deep brown in colour and the onion has softened.

Add vegetable stock and simmer until lentils are soft; about 30–45 minutes.

Remove cinnamon stick, whole green chilli and curry leaves.

Blend with a hand-held mixer or food processor until smooth, then return it to the pan.

Add diced vegetables and simmer for another 20 minutes or until vegetables are soft.

Add lemon juice, salt and chopped coriander. Stir well and serve with a dollop of yoghurt, garnished with a few extra coriander leaves.

SERVES 4

2 tbsp ghee or vegetable oil

350 g (12 oz) red lentils

1 tsp mustard seeds

1 tsp ground coriander

1 tsp ground cumin

1½ tsp turmeric

1 cinnamon stick

6 cloves garlic, crushed

1 tbsp root ginger, minced

10 fresh curry leaves, bruised and tied together

1 large onion, finely chopped

1 large green chilli, whole but split

2 l (3½ pints) rich vegetable stock

2 tomatoes, finely diced

1 small eggplant (aubergine), diced

1 small carrot, finely diced

1 large potato, peeled and diced

juice of 4 lemons

salt, to taste

1 bunch fresh coriander (cilantro)

4 tbsp natural (plain) yoghurt

Soups

Lamb with spiced rice

Lightly brown meat in butter. Add salt and spices and stir for 2 minutes.

Add the rice, stir and add the boiling chicken stock and mix well. Bring back to the boil.

Cover and simmer for 20–25 minutes or until rice is tender and stock is absorbed.

Let cool for 30 minutes and put in large serving dish, ready to serve. Serve with natural yoghurt if desired.

While the rice is cooling sauté the pine nuts in 3–4 tablespoons olive oil until light brown. Garnish rice and meat with the sautéed pine nuts and serve.

SERVES 6-8

750 g (1 lb 13 oz) lean lamb,
  finely chopped

60 g (2 oz) butter

2 tsp salt

½ tsp black pepper

½ tsp allspice

½ tsp ground nutmeg

¼ tsp ground cinnamon

¼ tsp ground saffron

450 g (1 lb) basmati rice

900 ml (1½ pt) chicken stock,
  boiling

90 g (3 oz) pine nuts

Fruity beef curry

Place beef in slow cooker with apple, apricots, sultanas or currants, orange zest, salt and pepper to taste, ginger, lemon juice and garlic.

Blend stock with curry powder, add to cooker and stir gently. Cook on low for approximately 6–8 hours or on high for 5–6 hours (time will vary depending on the meat). About 30 minutes before serving, stir in yoghurt and heat through. Serve with rice and chutney.

If preferred, beef may be browned first in a frying pan in a little oil. This improves the flavour and colour of the dish, but is not essential.

SERVES 4

500 g (1¼ lb) beef, cubed

1 large cooking apple, peeled and diced

115 g (4 oz) dried apricots, chopped

55 g (2 oz) sultanas (golden raisins) or currants

1 strip orange zest

salt and freshly ground black pepper

1 cm (½ in) piece fresh root ginger, grated

1 tbsp lemon juice

½ clove garlic, crushed

250 ml (8 fl oz) beef stock

1–2 tbsp curry powder

2 tbsp natural (plain) yoghurt

Indian meatballs in tomato sauce

SERVES 4

500 g (1 lb) lean lamb mince

125 g (4½ oz) natural yoghurt

5 cm (2 in) ginger, grated

1 green chilli, deseeded, finely
   chopped

10 g (½ oz) chopped fresh coriander
   (cilantro)

2 tsp ground cumin

2 tsp ground coriander

salt and freshly ground black
   pepper

2 tbsp olive oil

1 onion, chopped

2 cloves garlic, chopped

½ tsp ground turmeric

1 tsp garam masala

175 ml (6 fl oz) water

400 g (14 oz) canned chopped
   tomatoes

Combine the lamb, 1 tablespoon of yoghurt, ginger, chilli, 2 tablespoons of chopped fresh coriander, cumin and ground coriander in a large bowl and season with salt and pepper. Shape the mixture into 16 balls.

Heat 1 tablespoon of oil in a large saucepan, add meatballs and cook for 10 minutes, turning until browned (you may have to cook them in batches). Drain on absorbent paper and set aside.

In a slow cooker on a high setting add the remaining olive oil, onion and garlic and stir. Mix the turmeric and garam masala with 1 tablespoon of the water, then add to onion and garlic. Add remaining yoghurt, 1 tablespoon at a time, stirring well each time.

Add the tomatoes, meatballs and remaining water to the mixture and bring to temperature. Cook for 5 hours, stirring occasionally. Sprinkle over the rest of the cilantro to garnish and serve on a bed of rice.

Mince curry with peas & mint

In a large bowl, break up the mince thoroughly with your fingers. Add the water and stir to break up further (the water will evaporate while cooking). Mix in the salt, garlic, ginger, masala, turmeric and lemon juice.

To make the vagaar, heat the oil and spices in a large saucepan with a well-fitting lid. Add the onions, cover, reduce the heat and allow the onions to brown. Add the mince and braise for 5–7 minutes. Stir in the potatoes and carrots, then cover and cook for 30 minutes over a medium heat. Stir occasionally. Add the tomatoes, cover and cook for a further 10 minutes.

Garnish with the dhania and garam masala. Serve with warm roti, foolka bread or naan, and a dhania chutney.

Add the peas and mint to the basic mince mixture 15 minutes before the end of cooking but only after the tomatoes have been added and cooked for 10 minutes.

SERVES 6

1 kg (2 lbs) chicken mince

250 ml (8 fl oz) cold water

2 tsp salt

2 tsp fresh garlic, crushed

2½ tsp fresh ginger, crushed

1 tsp green masala

1 tsp turmeric

2 tsp lemon juice

VAGAAR

80 ml (3 fl oz) cooking oil

2 cinnamon sticks, each 5 cm (2 in)

4 whole cloves, 4 cardamom pods

2 onions, chopped

4 potatoes, 4 carrots, halved

2 tomatoes, chopped

2 tbsp coriander leaves, chopped

1 tsp garam masala

450 g (1 lb) frozen peas

3 tbsp fresh mint, chopped

Meats

Beef keema

SERVES 4

3 tbsp vegetable oil

2 onions, sliced

1 clove garlic, crushed

1 cm (½ in) fresh root ginger, finely grated (shredded)

500 g (1 lb) lean beef mince

10 g (½ oz) fresh coriander (cilantro), chopped

1 fresh red chilli, chopped

55 g (2 oz) natural (plain) yoghurt

400 g (14 oz) brown rice

1 L (1¾ pt) beef stock

2 whole cloves

1 cinnamon stick

Heat oil in a frying pan over a medium heat. Add onions, garlic and ginger and cook, stirring, for 3–4 minutes or until onions are golden and tender. Add beef and cook, stirring, for 5 minutes or until beef is well browned.

Stir coriander, chilli and yoghurt into beef mixture and cook for 1 minute. Remove pan from heat.

Place rice, stock, cloves and cinnamon stick in a large pan and bring to the boil over a medium heat. Reduce heat to simmering, cover and simmer for 45 minutes. Remove pan from heat and stand, covered, for 5 minutes.

Lightly fork onion and beef mixture through rice and heat over a low heat, stirring, for 4–5 minutes, until keema is heated through.

Creamy veal curry

Heat the oil in a large frying pan and brown the veal. Add onion and garlic and sauté, then add the curry powder and cook gently for a few minutes, stirring occasionally.

Transfer veal mixture to slowcooker and add the red pepper, bay leaves and stock. Cook on low for approximately 6 hours.

About half an hour before serving, stir in coconut milk or cream. Remove bay leaves and serve with cooked rice, garnished with coriander or parsley.

SERVES 4

1 tbsp vegetable oil

500 g (1 lb) stewing veal, cubed and trimmed

1 large white onion, sliced

½ clove garlic, crushed or chopped

1 tsp curry powder

1 large red pepper (capsicum), sliced

2 bay leaves

175 ml (6 fl oz) chicken or veal stock

120 ml (4 fl oz) fresh coconut milk or 50 ml (2 fl oz) canned coconut cream

Meats

Lamb & spinach curry

SERVES 4

2 tbsp vegetable oil

2 onions, chopped

2 cloves garlic, chopped

2.5 cm (1 in) piece ginger, finely
   chopped

1 cinnamon stick

¼ tsp ground cloves

3 cardamom pods

750 g (1 lb 13 oz) lamb, diced

1 tbsp ground cumin

1 tbsp ground coriander

80 g (3 oz) natural (plain) yoghurt

2 tbsp tomato paste

250 ml (8 fl oz) beef stock

salt and freshly ground black
   pepper

120 g (4 oz) baby spinach, chopped

2 tbsp blanched almonds, toasted

Heat the oil in a large heavy pan. Add onions, garlic, ginger, cinnamon, cloves and cardamom and cook for 5 minutes. Add the lamb and cook for 5 minutes, turning, until it begins to brown.

Transfer mixture to slowcooker set on high. Mix in the cumin and coriander, then add the yoghurt 1 tablespoon at a time, stirring well after each addition. Mix the tomato paste and stock together and add to the cooker. Season to taste, then reduce the heat to low and cook for 7 hours.

Stir in the spinach, cover and simmer for another 15 minutes or until the mixture has reduced slightly. Remove the cinnamon stick and the cardamom pods and mix in the almonds.

Serve with rice.

Madras curry

Place flour in a plastic bag and season with salt and pepper. Add stewing steak, close bag and shake until evenly coated.

Heat ghee or oil in a heavy pan, add floured beef cubes and fry for 5 minutes, stirring and turning meat so that all sides are browned.

Add onions and cook, stirring occasionally, for 5 minutes longer.

Stir in spices and cook for 3 minutes, then add garlic. Cook for 2 minutes. Add the hot water. Bring to the boil and boil briskly, stirring constantly, for 5 minutes.

Stir in raisins and add more water, if necessary, to cover meat. Bring to the boil, lower heat and simmer for 2¼ hours, adding more water as required. Serve at once or cool swiftly, refrigerate and reheat next day.

SERVES 4

30 g (1 oz) plain (all-purpose) flour

salt and freshly ground black
  pepper to taste

500 g (1 lb) stewing steak, cubed

55 g (2 oz) ghee or 4 tbsp oil

2 onions, finely chopped

1 tsp ground turmeric

1 tsp ground coriander

1 tsp cayenne pepper

½ tsp ground black mustard seeds

½ tsp ground cumin

2 cloves garlic, crushed

145 ml (5 fl oz) hot water

Meats

Lamb korma

SERVES 4–6

1½ kg (3½ lb) shoulder of lamb

salt and freshly ground black
   pepper

2 tbsp ghee

1 red onion, finely chopped

1 clove garlic, finely chopped

1 tbsp green masala paste

¼ tsp ground ginger

¼ tsp turmeric

1/8 tsp cayenne pepper

2 tbsp plain (all-purpose) flour

300 ml (10 fl oz) chicken stock

175 g (6 oz) sultanas (golden
   raisins)

145 ml (5 fl oz) natural
   (plain) yoghurt

1 tbsp lemon juice

rice and sambals, to serve

Cut lamb from bone and chop into 4 cm (1½ in) cubes.
Season with salt and pepper.

Heat ghee in a large, heavy pan, add one third of the
lamb and brown well on all sides. Remove and brown
remainder in two batches.

Add onion and garlic and sauté until transparent.
Stir in curry paste, spices and flour and cook for
1 minute. Add chicken stock, sultanas and lamb.
Cover with a lid and simmer gently for 1 hour or
until lamb is very tender. Stir occasionally during
cooking.

Stir in yoghurt and lemon juice. Serve with boiled
rice and sambals.

Pork vindaloo

Place pork in a pan with salt. Pour in water to cover meat by about 2.5 cm (1 in). Bring to the boil, lower heat and simmer for 45 minutes or until meat is tender.

Meanwhile, dry-fry chillies, cumin seeds, coriander seeds, cloves, peppercorns and cinnamon stick in a frying pan for a few minutes, until mixture starts to crackle. Don't let it burn.

Using a mortar and pestle, or a coffee grinder kept especially for the purpose, grind spices with ginger, garlic and vinegar to a smooth paste.

Heat oil in a large frying pan. Fry onions for about 10 minutes, until golden. Stir in spice paste and fry for 2 minutes more, stirring constantly.

Drain meat and reserve the cooking liquid, then add the pork to the frying pan. Stir well, cover and cook for 10 minutes over moderate heat. Add about 480 ml (16 fl oz) of reserved cooking liquid. Stir well, cover and cook for 15–20 minutes more, or until meat is coated in a thick spicy sauce.

Serve garnished with red chillies, or tip into a casserole, cool quickly, and refrigerate for reheating next day.

SERVES 4

500 g (1 lb) lean pork, cubed

pinch of salt

3 small dried red chillies

1 tsp cumin seeds

1½ tsp coriander seeds

2 cloves

6 black peppercorns

2.5 cm (1 in) cinnamon stick

2.5 cm (1 in) fresh root ginger, grated (shredded)

2 cloves garlic, chopped

3 tbsp vinegar

3 tbsp oil

2 onions, finely chopped

Meats

Poultry

Chicken rogan josh

SERVES 4

8 skinless chicken thigh fillets

1 tbsp vegetable oil

1 small red pepper/capsicum,
   thinly sliced

1 small green pepper (capsicum),
   thinly sliced

1 onion, thinly sliced

5 cm (2 in) piece fresh ginger, finely
   chopped

2 cloves garlic, crushed

2 tbsp garam masala

1 tsp paprika

1 tsp turmeric

1 tsp chilli powder

4 cardamom pods, crushed salt

200 g (7 oz) Greek yoghurt

400 g (14 oz) canned chopped
   tomatoes

fresh coriander (cilantro)
   to garnish

rice, yoghurt and chutney, to serve

Cut each chicken thigh into 4 pieces. Heat the oil in a large heavy-based frying pan and add the peppers, onion, ginger, garlic, spices and a good pinch of salt. Fry over a low heat for 5 minutes or until the pepper and onion have softened.

Add the chicken and 2 tablespoons of the yoghurt. Increase the heat to medium and cook for 4 minutes or until the yoghurt is absorbed. Repeat with the rest of the yoghurt.

Increase the heat to high, stir in the tomatoes and 175 ml (6 fl oz) of water and bring to the boil. Reduce the heat, cover, and simmer for 30 minutes or until the chicken is tender, stirring occasionally and adding more water if the sauce becomes too dry.

Uncover the pan, increase the heat to high and cook, stirring constantly, for 5 minutes or until the sauce thickens. Garnish with coriander and serve with rice, yoghurt and chutney.

Cashew nut butter chicken

Cut chicken into 2 cm (¾ in) cubes. Melt ghee in a saucepan over medium heat, add garlic and onion and cook, stirring, for 3 minutes or until onion turns golden.

Stir in curry paste, coriander and nutmeg and cook for 2 minutes or until fragrant.

Add chicken and cook, stirring, for 5 minutes or until chicken is brown.

Add cashews, cream and coconut milk and simmer, stirring occasionally, for 40 minutes or until chicken is tender.

To roast cashews, spread nuts over a baking tray and bake at 180°C/360°F for 5–10 minutes or until lightly and evenly browned. Toss back and forth occasionally with a spoon to ensure even browning. Alternatively, place nuts under a medium grill and cook, tossing back and forth until roasted.

SERVES 4

500 g (1 lb) skinless chicken thigh fillets

1¾ oz/50g ghee (clarified butter)

2 cloves garlic, crushed

2 onions, minced

1 tbsp Madras curry paste

1 tbsp ground coriander (cilantro)

½ tsp ground nutmeg

50 g (2 oz) cashew nuts, roasted and ground

300 ml (10 fl oz) double cream

2 tbsp coconut milk

Sweet mango chicken

SERVES 4

500 g (1 lb) chicken breast fillets

2 tbsp peanut oil

1 onion, cut into wedges

2 tsp mild curry powder

120 ml (4 fl oz) chicken stock

75 g (3 oz) mango chutney

10 g (½ oz) coriander
(cilantro) leaves

1 tsp mint flakes

1 small red pepper (capsicum),
sliced

100 g (3½ oz) baby spinach leaves,
washed and trimmed

40 g (1½ oz) cashew nuts, toasted

Pappadums and rice, to serve

Thickly slice the chicken breasts. Heat the oil in a large saucepan over high heat. Add the chicken and cook in two batches for 3 minutes. Remove and set aside.

Reduce the heat to medium, add the onion and cook for 2–3 minutes. Stir in the curry powder, chicken stock, mango chutney, coriander, mint, red pepper and chicken. Cook for 5–6 minutes or until the chicken is tender.

Stir through the spinach and cashews. Serve with pappadums and rice.

To toast cashew nuts, place on a baking tray lined with baking paper and bake at 180°C/360°F for 4–5 minutes or until golden. Alternatively, you can stir-fry in a pan until golden.

Tandoori wings

Combine marinade ingredients and mix well. Marinate chicken wings for at least 1 hour, ensuring each wing is well coated with the marinade.

Grill (broil) on high, turning occasionally or bake in oven on rack at 180°C/350°F for 20–25 minutes. Garnish with lemon.

SERVES 4-6

24 chicken wings

MARINADE

200 g (7 oz) natural (plain) yoghurt
5 tbsp tandoori paste
2 tbsp desiccated (dry, shredded unsweetened) coconut
lemon wedges, to garnish

Poultry

Masala duck curry

SERVES 4

1 tbsp sesame oil

2 kg (4½ lb) duck, cleaned and cut
  into 8 pieces

1 onion, chopped

2 small fresh red chillies, finely
  chopped, plus 2 sliced

1 stalk fresh lemongrass, bruised

2 tbsp green masala paste

350 ml (12 fl oz) coconut milk

3 fresh or dried curry leaves

1 tbsp lime juice

1 tbsp brown sugar

10 g (½ oz) coriander (cilantro)
  leaves, chopped

30 g (1 oz) fresh basil leaves

3 fresh green chillies, seeded and
  sliced

Heat the oil in a pan over medium heat. Add duck and cook, turning frequently, for 10 minutes or until brown on all sides. Remove and drain on kitchen paper.

Add onion, chopped red chillies and lemongrass to pan and cook, stirring, for 3 minutes or until onion is golden.

Stir in masala paste and cook for 2 minutes longer or until fragrant.

Stir in coconut milk, curry leaves, lime juice and sugar and return duck to pan. Bring to boil and simmer, stirring occasionally, for 45 minutes.

Add coriander, basil and sliced green and red chillies and cook for 10 minutes longer or until duck is tender. Remove lemongrass, then serve duck with green beans and rice.

Tikka skewers

Pierce tenderloins several times with a fork and place in a shallow ceramic or glass dish.

To make marinade, place onion, garlic, ginger, cumin, garam masala, cardamom, turmeric, chilli powder, coriander and tomato purée in a food processor or blender and process until smooth. Add yoghurt and mix to combine. Spoon marinade over chicken, toss to combine, cover and marinate in the refrigerator for 3 hours.

Preheat barbecue to a medium heat. Drain chicken and thread onto lightly oiled skewers. Place skewers on lightly oiled barbecue rack and cook, turning several times, for 5–6 minutes or until cooked.

To make raita, place cucumber, mint and yoghurt in a bowl and mix to combine. Serve skewers with lemon wedges and raita.

SERVES 4

500 g (1 lb) chicken tenderloins
oil, for cooking
1 lemon, cut into wedges

SPICY YOGHURT MARINADE

1 small onion, chopped
3 cloves garlic, crushed
1 cm (½ in) ginger, finely grated
1 tbsp ground cumin
1 tbsp garam masala
2 cardamom pods, crushed
1 tsp ground turmeric
1 tsp chilli powder
1 tsp ground coriander (cilantro)
1 tbsp tomato purée
275 g (10 oz) natural (plain) yoghurt

CUCUMBER RAITA

1 cucumber, finely chopped
10 g (½ oz) fresh mint, chopped
225 g (8 oz) natural (plain) yoghurt
Lemon wedges, to serve

Creamy chicken korma with rice

SERVES 4

3 tbsp vegetable oil

1 onion, chopped

2 cloves garlic, finely chopped

3 tbsp plain (all-purpose) flour

2 tbsp mild korma curry powder

750 g (1 lb 13 oz) skinless boneless chicken, cut into 2.5 cm (1 in) cubes

350 ml (12 fl oz) chicken stock

25 g (1 oz) raisins

1 tbsp fresh coriander (cilantro) chopped

1 tsp / 5 ml garam masala

juice of ½ lemon

4 tbsp soured cream

400 g (14 oz) steamed rice, to serve

Heat the oil in a large heavy pan, add the onion and garlic and cook gently for 5 minutes or until softened.

Put the flour and curry powder into a bowl and mix together. Toss the chicken in the seasoned flour, coating well. Reserve the flour. Add the chicken to the onion and garlic, then cook, stirring, for 3–4 minutes, until lightly browned. Stir in the seasoned flour and cook for 1 minute.

Add the stock and raisins and bring to the boil, stirring. Cover and simmer for 15 minutes.

Add the coriander and garam masala and cook for another 5 minutes or until the flavours are released and the chicken is cooked through. Remove the pan from the heat and stir in the lemon juice and soured cream. Return to the heat and warm through, taking care not to let the mixture boil. Serve with steamed rice.

Note: If you like curry but don't want to spend hours in the kitchen, you'll love this. It's quite mild and goes well with rice or chapattis. Try it with crispy fried onion rings.

Chicken curry with jasmine rice

Combine coconut milk, stock, curry paste and lime leaves in a slowcooker on high. Cook until the sauce begins to thicken. Add the pumpkin and cook for 20 minutes or until it starts to soften.

Add the chicken and bamboo shoots and cook for 1 hour. Add the beans, broccoli, fish sauce and palm sugar and cook until the vegetables are tender, for approximately 1 more hour. Then stir through the basil leaves.

Meanwhile, to make the jasmine rice, put the rice, lemongrass and water in a pot. Bring to boil and cook over a high heat until steam holes appear in the top of the rice. Reduce the heat to low, cover and cook for 10 minutes or until all the liquid is absorbed and the rice is tender. Transfer the rice to bowls, spoon over the curry and serve.

SERVES 4

480 ml (16 fl oz) reduced-fat coconut milk

240 ml (8 fl oz) reduced-salt chicken stock

2 tbsp green curry paste

3 kaffir lime leaves, shredded

200 g (7 oz) chopped pumpkin

4 skinless chicken breast fillets, diced

115 g (4 oz) canned bamboo shoots, drained

100 g (3½ oz) snake beans, chopped

200 g (7 oz) broccoli, cut into florets

1 tbsp fish sauce

1 tbsp grated palm sugar

2 tbsp torn fresh Thai basil leaves

JASMINE RICE

225 g (8 oz) jasmine rice

2 stalks lemongrass, halved

900 ml (1½ pt) water

Poultry

Chicken gado

SERVES 4

500 g (1 lb) chicken
   tenderloins
225 g (8 oz) medium-grain rice
200 g (7 oz) green beans,
   trimmed and halved
60 g (2 oz) roasted unsalted
   peanuts

SATAY MARINADE

90 g (3 oz) peanut butter
½ tsp chilli powder
½ tsp ground ginger
2 tbsp lemon juice
1 tbsp brown sugar
120 ml (4 fl oz) coconut milk

Place all marinade ingredients in a pan, heat and stir to combine. Place tenderloins in a non-metallic dish and stir in enough marinade to coat well. Cover and marinate at least 30 minutes in refrigerator.

Cook rice in boiling, salted water until tender, about 15 minutes. Drain well. Steam beans until tender but still crisp, then drain. Mix rice, beans and half the roasted peanuts together. Keep hot.

Heat the barbecue grill and add the tenderloins. Cook for 2 minutes on each side on high heat, brushing with marinade during cooking. Heat extra marinade on side of barbecue.

Pile rice into centre of heated plates. Arrange 2 or 3 tenderloins over the rice, top with heated marinade and sprinkle with remaining roasted peanuts.

Coconut fried chicken

Place chicken, coconut milk, onion, garlic, coriander, coconut, chilli, ginger, turmeric, cumin, sugar, lemon juice and lemon zest in a saucepan and bring to the boil over a medium heat. Reduce heat to simmering and simmer for 20 minutes or until chicken is just cooked and sauce is very thick.

Remove chicken from pan and drain. Reserve sauce and keep warm. Place chicken under a preheated hot grill and cook for 3–5 minutes each side or until golden and crisp. Combine brown rice and wild rice. Serve chicken on a bed of rice topped with reserved sauce.

SERVES 4

1 kg (2 lbs) chicken pieces

240 ml (8 fl oz) coconut milk

1 onion, chopped

2 cloves garlic, crushed

10 g (½ oz) fresh coriander (cilantro), chopped

1 tbsp desiccated coconut

1 large fresh red chilli, chopped

12 mm (½ in) (12mm) piece fresh ginger, finely grated

2 tsp ground turmeric

1 tsp ground cumin

1 tsp brown sugar

2 tbsp lemon juice

zest of ½ lemon, finely grated

200 g (7 oz) brown rice, cooked and kept warm

75 g (3 oz) wild rice, cooked and kept warm

Poultry

Rice & apricot pilaf

SERVES 4

3 tbsp oil or butter

1 large onion, finely chopped

225 g (8 oz) rice

900 ml (1½ pt) hot water

salt and freshly ground pepper

*2 tbsp parsley, finely
chopped*

2 tbsp lemon juice

200 g (7 oz) dried apricots

2 tbsp seedless raisins

*60 g (2 oz) almonds, blanched
    and toasted*

In a large saucepan heat oil or butter and fry the onion until pale golden in colour. Add the rice and stir 30 seconds to coat with oil.

Add the hot water, salt, pepper, parsley and lemon juice. Cover and simmer for 10 minutes.

Stir in the apricots (whole), raisins and almonds and simmer for 5 minutes more. Remove from heat and allow to stand, covered, for 5 minutes before serving.

Root Vegetable Curry

Heat the oil in a large saucepan. Add the onion, chilli, garlic and ginger and cook for 5 minutes or until softened, stirring occasionally. Stir in the flour, ground coriander, cumin and turmeric and cook gently, stirring, for 1 minute to release the flavours.

Gradually stir in the stock, then add the tomato purée, cubed root vegetables and the carrots, season with black pepper and mix well.

Bring to the boil, stirring, then cover, reduce the heat and simmer for 45 minutes or until the vegetables are tender, stirring occasionally. Garnish with fresh coriander.

SERVES 4

1 tbsp olive oil

1 onion, chopped

1 green chilli, deseeded and finely chopped

1 clove garlic, finely chopped

2.5 cm (1 in) piece fresh root ginger, finely chopped

2 tbsp plain (all-purpose) flour

2 tsp each ground coriander, ground cumin and turmeric

300 ml (10 fl oz) vegetable stock

200 ml (7 fl oz) tomato purée

750 g (1lb 13 oz) mixed root vegetables, such as potato, sweet potato, celeriac and swede, cubed

2 carrots, thinly sliced

black pepper

chopped fresh coriander (cilantro) garnish

Vegetarian

Bombay hot lentils

SERVES 4

200 g (7 oz) mung dhal (small
*   yellow lentils), soaked*

½ tsp ground turmeric

2.5 cm (1 in) piece fresh ginger,
*   finely chopped*

1 tbsp vegetable oil

salt and black pepper

1 tbsp tamarind

1 tbsp brown sugar

½ bunch fresh coriander (cilantro),

3 tbsp flaked coconut

2 tsp garam masala

WHOLE SPICE MIXTURE

85 g (3 oz) ghee or butter

1 tsp cumin seeds

1 tsp black mustard seeds

¼ tsp fenugreek seeds

2 tbsp chopped curry leaves

3 red or green chillies, chopped fine

5 cm (2 in) ginger, finely chopped

salt

Place 480 ml (16 fl oz) water in a large pan and bring to the boil. Stir in lentils, turmeric, ginger, oil, salt and pepper to taste and cook over a low heat, stirring occasionally for 30–45 minutes or until lentils are very soft. Remove pan from heat and mash lentil mixture.

Place tamarind in a small bowl, pour over 250 ml (8 fl oz) hot water and set aside to soak for 20 minutes. Drain liquid from tamarind mixture, then push tamarind pulp through a fine sieve (strainer) and set aside. Reserve juice for another use.

For spice mixture, heat ghee or butter in a large pan, add remaining ingredients and cook, stirring for 1 minute.

Add lentil mixture and 1 litre (1¾ pints) water to spice mixture and bring to the boil. Stir tamarind pulp and brown sugar into lentil mixture and cook, stirring occasionally for 5 minutes longer.

Stir in coriander, coconut and garam masala and cook for 2 minutes longer.

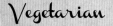

Split lentil dhal with ginger & coriander

Rinse the lentils and drain well, then place in a large pan with 900 ml (1½ pints) of water. Bring to the boil, skimming any scum, then stir in the turmeric. Reduce the heat and partly cover the pan. Simmer for 30–35 minutes, stirring occasionally, until thickened.

Heat the oil in a small frying pan, then add the ginger and cumin seeds and fry for 30 seconds or until the cumin seeds start to pop. Stir in the ground coriander and cook for 1 minute.

Season the lentils with plenty of salt and pepper, then add the toasted spices. Stir in the chopped coriander, mixing well. Transfer to a serving dish and garnish with the paprika and extra coriander leaves.

Note: Dhal is very much an everyday dish in Indian households. Ginger and fresh coriander add extra zest to this version of the slowly simmered lentil purée.

SERVES 4

200 g (7 oz) dried split red lentils

½ tsp turmeric

1 tbsp vegetable oil

1 cm (½ in) piece fresh ginger, finely chopped

1 tsp cumin seeds

1 tsp ground coriander

salt and freshly ground black pepper

10 g (½ oz) fresh coriander (cilantro), chopped

½ tsp paprika

Vegetarian

Bean curry

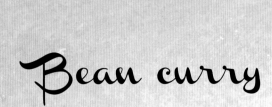

SERVES 4

1 onion, peeled

5 cm (2 in) piece fresh root ginger,
  peeled

2 cloves garlic, peeled

1 tbsp olive oil

2 tsp curry powder

1 tsp ground cumin

1 tsp turmeric

75 g (3 oz) sweet fruit chutney

60 g (2 oz) crunchy peanut butter

400 g (14 oz) can peeled tomatoes

60 g (2 oz) tomato paste

400 g (14 oz) can cannellini beans,
  drained

400 g (14 oz) can borlotti beans,
  drained

Place roughly chopped onion, ginger and garlic in processor and blend until smooth.

Heat oil in pan, cook onion mixture, stirring occasionally for 5 minutes, add curry, cumin and turmeric and cook, stirring for 1 minute.

Add chutney, peanut butter, tomatoes, tomato paste, 250 ml (8 fl oz) of water and beans. Stir until well combined. Bring to boil, reduce heat and simmer covered 20 minutes. Serve with rice.

Vegetarian

Vegetable & lentil curry

Heat oil in a large pan, add onion, garlic, cumin, coriander, turmeric and carrots and cook for 5 minutes or until onion is soft.

Stir in lentils, tomatoes and stock or water and bring to the boil. Reduce heat, cover and simmer for 15 minutes.

Add chilli sauce, pumpkin or potatoes and cauliflower and cook for 15–20 minutes longer or until pumpkin or potatoes are tender. Stir in almonds and black pepper to taste. To serve, ladle curry into bowls and top with a spoonful of yoghurt.

SERVES 4

1 tbsp olive oil

1 onion, sliced

1 clove garlic, crushed

1 tsp ground cumin

1 tsp ground coriander

1 tsp ground turmeric

2 carrots, sliced

100 g (3½ oz) red lentils

200 g (7 oz) can tomatoes, mashed
*   with the juice*

350 ml (12 fl oz) vegetable stock
*   or water*

1 tsp chilli sauce

450 g (1 lb) pumpkin or potatoes,
*   cut into 2.5 cm / 1 in cubes*

½ cauliflower, cut into florets

2 tbsp blanched almonds

freshly ground black pepper

4 tbsp natural yoghurt

Vegetarian

Vegetable korma

SERVES 4

2 tbsp vegetable oil

2 tbsp green masala curry paste

1 tsp chilli powder

1 tbsp fresh ginger, finely grated
  (shredded)

2 cloves garlic, crushed

1 onion, chopped

500 g (1 lb) cauliflower, cut into
  florets

200 g (7 oz) green beans

3 baby eggplants (aubergines)

2 carrots, sliced

125 g (4½ oz) button (white)
  mushrooms

400 g (14 oz) can tomatoes, mashed
  in their juices

250 ml (8 fl oz) vegetable stock

Heat oil in a pan over medium heat, stir in masala paste and chilli powder and cook for 2 minutes. Add ginger, garlic and onion and cook, stirring, for 3 minutes or until onion is soft. Add cauliflower, beans, eggplants, carrots and mushrooms and cook, stirring, for 5 minutes.

Stir in tomatoes and stock, and bring to the boil. Reduce heat and simmer, stirring occasionally, for 20 minutes or until vegetables are tender.

Lentil burger

To make sauce, place yoghurt and mint in a small bowl and mix to combine.

Put red lentils in a pan, cover with cold water and bring to the boil. Cook for 15–20 minutes, or until the lentils are soft. Drain the lentils and mash.

Place potatoes in a large pan, cover with cold water and bring to the boil. Simmer uncovered for 20–30 minutes or until potatoes are soft to the centre. Drain the potatoes and return to the pan over low heat, allowing the potatoes to steam for a few minutes. Add milk and butter and mash until creamy.

Place lentils, mashed potato, milk, egg, spring onions, garlic, cumin, coriander, curry powder and black pepper to taste in a bowl and mix to combine.

Shape lentil mixture into eight patties and cook under a preheated grill (broiler) for 5 minutes each side or until golden and heated through.

Place a warm burger between the pieces of each toasted roll, add sauce and serve.

SERVES 4

90 g (3 oz) red lentils, cooked, drained and mashed

250 g (9 oz) potatoes, peeled and mashed

2 tbsp butter

175 ml (6 fl oz) milk

1 egg, lightly beaten

4 spring onions (scallions), chopped

1 clove garlic, crushed

1 tsp ground cumin

1 tbsp fresh coriander (cilantro), chopped

1 tsp curry powder

freshly ground black pepper

4 bread rolls, split and toasted

Yoghurt MINT SAUCE

225 g (8 oz) natural (plain) yoghurt

1 tbsp fresh mint, chopped

Vegetarian

Okra & chickpea salad

SERVES 4

180 g (6 oz) dried chickpeas
  (garbanzos)
1½ tbsp olive oil
1 medium red onion, cut into 8
  wedges
1 clove garlic, crushed
300 g (10½ oz) pickled okra,
  drained
3 tomatoes, skinned and quartered
4 tbsp chopped fresh coriander
  (cilantro)
1½ tbsp lemon juice
freshly ground black pepper
25 g (1 oz) fresh mint leaves

Place chickpeas in a bowl, cover with cold water and set aside to soak overnight.

Drain and place in a large pan with enough cold water to cover chickpeas by 5 cm (2 in). Bring to the boil and boil rapidly for 5 minutes, then reduce heat and simmer for 1½ hours or until chickpeas are tender. Drain, and reserve 4 tbsp of cooking liquid.

Heat the oil in a large frying pan and cook onion over a low heat for 10 minutes or until golden. Add garlic, okra, chickpeas and reserved cooking liquid and cook for 4–5 minutes or until okra is tender.

Add tomatoes, coriander, lemon juice and black pepper to taste, add mint and toss to combine. Serve hot or cold.

Note: Okra, also known as gumbo and lady's fingers, is a close relative of the ornamental hibiscus. When buying okra, choose crisp, young, small pods. When cooked, okra should be soft but still have just a little of its crunch.

Red Snapper with Coconut Sauce

Combine all ingredients except snapper in a food processor and blend to a smooth paste.

Divide fish into four even portions. Remove any major bones. Score skin of fish with a sharp knife.

Smear paste onto snapper, pressing into slits. Set aside for cooking.

Prepare coconut sauce by combining coconut milk, lime juice, palm sugar and fish sauce in a small saucepan. Heat until warm and sugar has dissolved.

Heat a little oil in a frying pan until almost smoking and add fish, skin-side down. Cook until golden brown, about 2 minutes on each side.

Serve with coconut sauce and Asian greens.

SERVES 4

600 g (1 lb 5 oz) red snapper

2 stalks lemongrass, very finely sliced

2 cm (¾ in) piece galangal, grated

6 cloves garlic, roughly chopped

1 French shallot, roughly chopped

2 small red chillies, deseeded

2 kaffir lime leaves

10 g (½ oz) dill

1 tbsp sesame seeds

COCONUT SAUCE

480 ml (16 fl oz) coconut milk

juice of 2 limes

2 tbsp palm sugar

1 tbsp fish sauce

Seafood

Goan seafood curry

SERVES 6

500 g (1 lb) tiger prawns (shrimp)

250 g (9 oz) firm fish

6 crayfish tails

2 tsp salt

1 tsp turmeric

1 tsp paprika (or chilli powder)

1 tsp lemon juice, 1 tsp cooking oil

2 tbsp desiccated coconut

6 large ripe tomatoes, skinned

3 tbsp ghee, 2 tbsp cooking oil

2 large onions, finely chopped

2 tsp fresh garlic, pounded

1 tsp fresh ginger, pounded

10 curry leaves

1 tsp red chilli powder or paprika

½ tsp turmeric

1–2 green chillies, sliced lengthwise

1 tsp aniseed, crushed

2 tsp sugar

3 tbsp coriander (cilantro) leaves

2 tbsp tomato paste

250 ml (8 fl oz) coconut cream

Rinse the shrimp in cold water. Remove the heads and pinch off the claws. De-vein the shrimp. Cut the fish into 5 cm (2 in) pieces, sprinkle with salt and wash with cold water. Clean the crayfish tails similarly and de-vein them. Leave the bright shells on. Place the seafood in a bowl and rub in 1 tsp salt, turmeric and paprika. Add lemon juice and oil, then leave to rest for 1 hour.

Soak the coconut in 250 ml (8 fl oz) warm water. Cut the tomatoes into wedges. Heat the ghee and cooking oil in a large pan. Fry the onions until brown. Add the garlic, ginger and pinch of salt, then stir for 2 minutes. Stir in the coconut with the water. Add the curry leaves, chilli powder, turmeric, green chillies, aniseed, sugar and 2 tablespoons of the coriander leaves. Cook, covered, for 15 minutes.

Stir in the tomato paste. Cook for another 15 minutes to reduce the sauce. (Cook until the oil rises to the surface in small bubbles.) Stir in the cream. Gently add the seafood, cover, and leave to simmer for another 15 minutes. Garnish with the remaining coriander, and serve with rice, salad and a tomato relish or yoghurt.

Curried scallops

Place scallops, white wine and bouquet garni in the slow cooker and cook on low for approximately 1 hour. Pour off and reserve liquid, discard bouquet garni and keep scallops warm in slow cooker.

Put cooking liquid with butter into a small pan and boil hard to reduce. Stir in the cream, curry powder and salt and pepper, and again boil hard for 2–3 minutes. Remove from heat and allow to cool.

Beat egg yolks with milk, and carefully stir into cooled cream mixture. Pour mixture back into slow cooker with the scallops and cook on high for 45–60 minutes. To serve, place a little cooked rice in a small bowl and spoon over 3–4 scallops with a generous quantity of sauce. Serve immediately.

SERVES 6

250 g (9 oz) scallops

120 ml (4 fl oz) dry white wine

1 bouquet garni

115 g (4 oz) butter

250 ml (8 fl oz) single (light) cream

½ tsp curry powder

salt and freshly ground black pepper

2 egg yolks

2 tbsp milk

Seafood

Curry mussels

SERVES 4

2 tbsp olive oil

1 small onion, chopped

1 stalk celery, sliced

1 clove garlic, chopped

2 tbsp yellow curry paste

2 cardamom pods, crushed

pinch of ground cumin

1 kg (2 lbs) mussels, cleaned

55 ml (2 fl oz) coconut cream

10 g (½ oz) fresh coriander
(cilantro), chopped

1 red chilli, chopped, optional

Put oil, onion, celery, garlic, curry paste, cardamom and cumin in a pan and cook over a slow heat for 5 minutes, stirring frequently.

Add mussels and coconut cream and increase heat to high. Cook until all mussels have opened, stirring frequently to ensure mussels are cooked evenly. Discard any mussels that do not open.

Add coriander, stir and serve. Add chopped chilli if you like your curry very spicy.

Chilli sesame shrimp kebabs

Place oil, curry paste, ginger, garlic, lime juice and yoghurt in a bowl and mix to combine. Add shrimp and toss to coat. Cover and marinate in the refrigerator for 2–3 hours.

Drain shrimps and thread three shrimps onto an oiled skewer. Repeat with remaining shrimps to make twelve kebabs. Toss kebabs in sesame seeds and cook on a lightly oiled, preheated medium barbecue or under a grill (broiler) for 3 minutes each side or until shrimps are cooked.

To make masala onions, melt ghee or butter in a pan over a medium heat, add onions and cook, stirring, for 5 minutes or until soft. Stir in masala paste and cook for 2 minutes longer or until heated through. Serve with shrimps.

SERVES 6

1 tbsp vegetable oil

1 tbsp Madras curry paste

2 tbsp fresh ginger, grated (shredded)

2 cloves garlic, crushed

2 tbsp lime juice

115 g (4 oz) natural (plain) yoghurt

36 uncooked medium shrimp (prawns), shelled and deveined, tails intact

6 tbsp sesame seeds, toasted

GREEN MASALA ONIONS

30 g (1 oz) ghee or butter

2 onions, cut into wedges

2 tbsp green Masala paste

Seafood

Seafood Rice with Chilli Lime Butter

SERVES 4

200 g (7 oz) basmati rice

16 large raw shrimp (prawns)

2 tsp olive oil

100 g (3½ oz) butter, melted

1 red chilli, finely sliced

1 green chilli, finely sliced

1 small red onion, finely sliced

*1 lime, peeled and cut into small
    dice*

juice of 1 lime

*20 g (¾ oz) fresh coriander
    (cilantro), chopped*

Combine the rice with 480 ml (16 fl oz) water in a saucepan. Bring to the boil, reduce heat to low, cover and cook for 15 minutes, then allow to stand covered for 10 minutes.

Shell the shrimps, leaving the tails intact. To butterfly the shrimps, cut along the back, about halfway through. Remove the vein.

Heat the oil in a heavy-based frying pan, add the shrimps and cook until they change colour and are just cooked through. Set aside and keep warm.

Return pan to heat, add butter, chillies and onion. Sauté for 1–2 minutes, then add cooked rice and chopped lime and mix well. Add shrimps, season with lime juice, stir through coriander and serve.

Poached Salmon and Citrus Rice

Preheat oven to 200°C/400°F. Combine the rice with 480 ml (16 fl oz) water in a saucepan. Bring to the boil, reduce heat to low, cover and cook for 15 minutes. Remove pan from heat, stir through lemon juice and parsley. Stand covered for 10 minutes.

Meanwhile, place the salmon portions on a single sheet of baking paper. Top with lemon zest and finely sliced vegetables, season with salt and pepper and drizzle with white wine. Fold the sides of the baking paper together to form a tight parcel. Bake for 10–12 minutes.

Remove salmon from the parcel, top with baked vegetables and dill. Carefully pour over juices that have collected in the bag. Serve with citrus rice.

SERVES 4

200 g (7 oz) brown rice

zest and juice of 1 lemon

20 g (¾ oz) parsley, finely chopped

4 salmon fillets, about 200 g (7 oz) each

1 carrot, cut into matchsticks

1 stalk celery, cut into thin strips

1 green capsicum (bell pepper), cut into thin strips

salt and freshly ground black pepper

60 ml (2 fl oz) white wine

small bunch dill, roughly chopped

Seafood

Kedgeree

Place smoked fish in saucepan, cover with cold water and bring slowly to the simmer. Cook for 6 minutes, drain and flake.

Melt butter in a large frying pan over a medium heat and fry onion until soft. Add curry powder and cook, stirring, for 2 minutes. Add rice and leeks and fry gently for 5 minutes, stirring, until rice is translucent yet slightly brown in colour.

Place rice mixture in a slow cooker and add boiling water, dashi stock and flaked fish. Gently stir to combine all ingredients, cover and cook on high for 2 hours.

When ready to serve add cream and eggs and toss gently with a fork. Season to taste with freshly ground black pepper. Sprinkle with parsley. Serve with lemon wedges if desired.

SERVES 4

500 g (1 lb) smoked trout or cod

1 leek, diced, washed

30 g (1 oz) butter

1 onion, finely sliced

1 tsp curry powder

200 g (7 oz) basmati rice

480 ml (16 fl oz) boiling water

1 sachet Japanese dashi stock

2 tbsp cream

*2 hard-boiled eggs, coarsely
   chopped*

freshly ground black pepper

2 tbsp chopped fresh parsley

Sour shrimp curry

Place the coconut milk, shrimp paste, curry paste, lemongrass, chillies, cumin and coriander in a slow cooker set on high and bring to a simmer. Stirring occasionally, cook for 1 hour.

Stir the shrimp, cucumbers, bamboo shoots and tamarind mixture into the coconut milk mixture and cook, stirring occasionally, for 45 minutes or until the shrimp are cooked.

Serve with steamed rice.

SERVES 4

480 ml (16 fl oz) coconut milk

1 tsp shrimp paste

2 tbsp Thai green curry paste

1 stalk lemongrass, finely chopped
or ½ tsp dried lemongrass,
soaked in hot water until soft

2 fresh green chillies, chopped

1 tbsp ground cumin

1 tbsp ground coriander

500 g (1 lb) large uncooked
shrimp (prawns), shelled,
deveined (leaving tails intact)

3 cucumbers, halved and sliced

115 g (4 oz) canned bamboo shoots,
drained

1 tbsp tamarind concentrate,
dissolved in 3 tbsp hot water

Seafood

Goan-style fish & coconut curry

SERVES 4

2 tomatoes

2 cardamom pods, bruised

1 tsp ground coriander

1 tsp ground cumin

1 tsp ground cinnamon

1 tsp hot chilli powder

½ tsp ground turmeric

2 tbsp water

2 tbsp vegetable oil

1 onion, finely chopped

1 clove garlic, finely chopped

2.5 cm (1 in) piece fresh root ginger,
   finely chopped

14fl oz (400ml) coconut milk

24oz (700g) skinless white fish
   fillet, such as haddock or cod, cut
   into 2.5 cm (1 in) chunks

salt to taste

fresh coriander (cilantro) leaves to
   garnish

Place tomatoes in a bowl, cover with boiling water and leave to stand for 30 seconds. Peel, then finely chop.

Crush cardamom seeds using a mortar and pestle. Add coriander, cumin, cinnamon, chilli powder, turmeric and water and mix to a paste. Set aside.

Heat oil in a large heavy-based saucepan. Cook onion, garlic and ginger for 3 minutes or until softened. Add spice paste, mix well and cook for 1 minute, stirring constantly.

Transfer to a slow cooker on a high setting, pour in coconut milk and simmer for 30 minutes. Add fish, tomatoes and salt. Partly cover and cook for a further 45 minutes or until fish turns opaque and is cooked through. Garnish with coriander leaves and serve on a bed of rice.

Shrimp with basil and rice

Heat 1 tablespoon of the oil in a large frying pan. Add beaten egg and cook 1–2 minutes each side, remove from pan and cut into thin strips.

Heat remaining 1 tablespoon oil in pan, add onion and garlic and fry for 2 minutes. Stir in shrimp paste, mixing well.

Add all remaining ingredients and cook for 2–3 minutes, stirring occasionally. Serve topped with the sliced egg.

SERVES 4-6

2 tbsp oil

1 egg, lightly beaten

1 onion, chopped

2 cloves garlic, chopped

2 tsp shrimp paste

1 large tomato, chopped

2 spring onions (scallions), sliced

2 tbsp oyster sauce

800 g (1 lb 15 oz) cooked long-grain rice

15 fresh basil leaves

375 g (13 oz) cooked school shrimp (prawns), peeled

Seafood

Saffron rice with seafood

SERVES 4

good pinch of saffron

700 ml (1¼ pint) fish or chicken
* stock*

2 tbsp olive oil

2 onions, chopped

250 g (9 oz) long-grain rice, rinsed

250 g (9 oz) raw shrimp
(prawns), shelled and
deveined

250 g (9 oz) scallops

12 mussels or baby clams,
* cleaned*

small bunch coriander (cilantro)

Heat the saffron in the stock and leave to infuse. Heat the olive oil in a frying pan, paella or flattish casserole dish and gently cook the onions until soft and golden. Add the rice and cook, stirring until well coated with oil. Add the hot stock, stirring until mixture comes to the boil, then reduce the heat and simmer gently for 10 minutes.

Add the shrimp and scallops, pressing gently into the rice. Continue to cook for 5 minutes. Add the mussels or clams, which should open with the heat. If you have a lid, partly cover the rice. When the rice is tender (about 18–20 minutes) remove from the heat and gently fluff up the rice with a fork. Sprinkle cilantro over and serve.

Side Dishes

Chapatis

Sift flour and salt into a bowl. Make a well in the centre and add 250 ml (8 fl oz) of water, a little at a time, using your fingers to incorporate the surrounding flour to make a smooth, pliable dough.

Knead dough on a lightly floured surface for 5–10 minutes, then place in a bowl, cover with a cloth and leave to rest for 30–60 minutes.

Knead dough for 2–3 minutes. Divide into 6 balls of equal size, then flatten each ball a circle, about 13 cm (5 in) in diameter.

Heat a dry frying pan until hot. Place one chapati at a time on the hot surface. As soon as bubbles appear on the surface of the chapati, turn the bread over. Press down on chapati with a thick cloth so that it cooks evenly.

Remove with a fish slice and hold each carefully over an open gas flame without turning until it puffs up slightly. Alternatively, place the chapati under a hot grill (broiler).

Repeat with remaining dough circles. Keep cooked chapatis hot in a covered napkin-lined basket.

MAKES 15

*250 g (9 oz) wholemeal
(wholewheat) flour*

1 tsp salt

Side Dishes

Indian fresh corn bread

MAKES 4

250 g (9 oz) fresh corn kernels

½ tsp salt

2 tbsp ground (minced) coriander

145 g (5 oz) plain (all-purpose)
   flour, plus extra for dusting

1–2 tbsp ghee, melted

In a blender or food processor, grind corn and salt together until it is a fine powder.

Transfer mixture to a bowl and add coriander. Add flour, a little at a time, continuing until mixture is kneadable (it should be a little tacky).

Divide dough into 12 pieces, then roll each piece into a circle about 15 cm (6 in) diameter. If dough circles are too tacky, use extra flour to absorb dough moisture. Once rolled, brush each with a little ghee.

Heat a griddle or frying pan and add a little ghee. Add one piece of dough and cook until dough underside is spotted with brown. Turn and cook other side. Remove cooked bread and keep warm in foil while cooking other breads the same way.

Note: While many Westerners are unfamiliar with the breads of India, there are dozens of delicious and flavoursome varieties. This unusual yeast-free bread is from the area of Rajasthan in the west of the country.

If you would like to duplicate the smoky roasted flavour that these breads would have when cooked over an open fire, simply hold each bread over a gas flame for a few seconds. Do not allow to burn. Brush with more ghee and serve.

Roasted red pepper raita

Heat the grill (broiler) to high. Cut the red peppers lengthwise into quarters, then remove the seeds and grill (broil), skin-side up, for 10 minutes or until blackened and blistered. Place in a plastic bag, seal and leave to cool for 10 minutes.

Toast the cumin seeds in a small frying pan, stirring constantly over medium to high heat, until aromatic. Remove and reserve.

Peel the skins from the grilled pepper and discard, then roughly chop the flesh. Mix the pepper with the yoghurt, cumin seeds and mint and season to taste. Transfer to a serving dish and garnish with the paprika.

Note: Red pepper adds a slight sweetness to this cooling side dish. It can be made the day before and kept in refrigerated.

SERVES 4

2 red peppers (capsicum)

2 tsp cumin seeds

200 g (7 oz) Greek (strained plain) yoghurt

2 tbsp fresh mint, finely chopped

salt and freshly ground black pepper

1 tsp paprika, to garnish

Side Dishes

Fragrant pilau rice

SERVES 4

large pinch of saffron strands

225 g (8 oz) basmati rice

25 g (1 oz) butter

*1 spring onion (scallion), finely
 chopped*

3 cardamom pods

1 cinnamon stick

salt

Briefly grind the saffron using a mortar and pestle, then mix the powder with 1 tablespoon of boiling water and set aside. Rinse the rice and drain.

Melt the butter in a large, heavy pan. Fry the spring onion gently for 2 minutes or until softened. Add the cardamom pods, cinnamon and rice and mix well.

Add 300 ml (10 fl oz) of water, the saffron mixture and salt. Bring to the boil, then reduce the heat and cover the pan tightly. Simmer the rice for 15 minutes or until the liquid has been absorbed and the rice is tender. Remove the cardamom pods and cinnamon stick before serving.

Coconut sambal

Mix coconut, onion and chilli in a small bowl. Add lime juice, toss lightly and serve.

SERVES 4

55 g (2 oz) desiccated (dry unsweetened shredded) coconut

1 tbsp onion, finely chopped

1 small red chilli, seeded and chopped

1 tbsp lime juice

Side Dishes

Yoghurt and Cucumber Dip

SERVES 6–8

250 g (9 oz) plain yoghurt

1 medium cucumber

1 clove garlic, crushed

1 tbsp olive oil

1 tsp dill, chopped

2 tsp lemon juice

salt to taste

selection of crackers

Drain yoghurt by placing in a muslin-lined strainer over a bowl for at least an hour.

Wash and grate the cucumber and drain as above. Combine yoghurt, cucumber and garlic and gradually beat in olive oil, add remaining ingredients.

Chill then serve with a selection of cracker biscuits.

Green masala curry paste

Place soaked fenugreek seeds, garlic, ginger, coriander, mint and vinegar in a food processor or blender and process to make a smooth paste. Add fish sauce, turmeric and cardamom and process to combine.

Heat the sesame and vegetable oils together in a small pan over a medium heat for 5 minutes or until hot. Stir in paste and cook, stirring constantly, for 5 minutes or until mixture boils and thickens.

MAKES ABOUT 250 ML (8 FL OZ)

1 tsp fenugreek seeds, soaked in cold water overnight

3 cloves garlic, crushed

2 tbsp fresh ginger, grated (shredded)

40 g (1½ oz) (fresh coriander (cilantro), chopped

40 g (1½ oz) fresh mint, chopped

100 ml (3½ fl oz) vinegar

1 tsp Thai fish sauce (nam pla)

2 tsp ground turmeric

1 tsp ground cardamom

50 ml (2 fl oz) sesame oil

100 ml (3½ fl oz) vegetable oil

Side Dishes

Garam masala

Heat a heavy frying pan over moderate heat. Add the cardamom seeds, cumin seeds, coriander seeds, peppercorns, cloves and cinnamon stick. Cook, stirring, until evenly browned. Allow to cool.

Using a mortar and pestle, or a coffee grinder kept especially for the purpose, grind the roasted spices to a fine powder. Add nutmeg and mix well.

MAKES 4 TBSP/80 ML

2 tsp cardamom seeds

2 tsp cumin seeds

2 tsp coriander seeds

1 tsp black peppercorns

1 tsp whole cloves 1 cinnamon stick, broken

½ nutmeg, grated (shredded)

Aadoo mirch spice mix

Grind ginger and garlic in a blender or food processor, or use a mortar and pestle. Add the chillies and salt. Purée to a smooth paste, scrape into a bowl and cover tightly. Will keep for 1 week in the refrigerator.

MAKES 4 TBSP/80 ML

4 tbsp fresh ginger, grated (shredded)

1 clove garlic, chopped

12 small fresh chillies, chopped

½ tsp salt

Salads

Curried chicken salad

SERVES 4

1 cooked chicken

2 stalks celery, finely chopped

6 spring onions (scallions), sliced

50 g (2 oz) raisins, soaked

60 g (2 oz) slivered almonds,
  toasted

200 g (7 oz) mixed salad greens

DRESSING

110 g (4 oz) mayonnaise

125 g (4½ oz) low-fat yoghurt

3 tbsp sweet mango chutney

1 tbsp mild curry paste

2 tbsp lemon juice

zest of 2 lemons, grated

fresh fruit and toasted shredded

coconut, to serve (optional)

Remove the chicken meat from the bones and cut into bite-size pieces. Toss with the celery, spring onions, raisins and almonds. Place all dressing ingredients in a bowl and whisk until smooth.

Pour dressing over chicken, toss to mix through. Cover and chill 2 hours or more. Line platter or individual plates with salad greens and pile on the chicken mixture.

Garnish with fresh fruits of your choice (we used mango). Sprinkle top of salad with toasted shredded coconut.

Moghul salad

Place bean sprouts, cucumbers, coconut, tomatoes, coriander, mint and basil leaves, spring onions, lemon juice, and salt and black pepper in a bowl and toss to combine. Cover and stand at room temperature for 2–3 hours before serving.

SERVES 6

200 g (7 oz) mung bean sprouts

3 cucumbers, diced

1 tbsp grated (shredded) fresh or desiccated (dry, unsweetened shredded) coconut

2 tomatoes, diced

¼ bunch fresh coriander (cilantro) leaves, chopped

½ bunch fresh mint leaves, chopped

½ bunch fresh basil leaves, chopped

1 bunch spring onions (scallions), chopped

2 tbsp lemon juice

salt and freshly ground black pepper

Salads

Chicken salad with mixed wild rice

SERVES 6-8

1 kg (2 lbs) lean chicken, diced

1 tsp salt, 1 tsp pepper

1 tsp paprika

1 tsp ground cumin

1 tsp onion powder

480 ml (16 fl oz) orange juice

60 ml (2 fl oz) dry white wine

2 onions, diced

60 g (2 oz) apricot jelly

60 g (2 oz) peach jelly

90 g (3 oz) honey

2 tbsp lemon juice

2 tbsp lime juice

500 g (1 lb) fresh kumquats

40 g (1½ oz) wild rice

75 g (3 oz) brown rice

150 g (5 oz) white rice

1 bunch basil, leaves thinly sliced

*125 g (4 oz) toasted pistachio nuts,
   chopped*

Place the diced chicken in a plastic bag and add the salt, pepper, paprika, ground cumin, and onion powder and seal the bag. Shake to coat the chicken, then thread the chicken pieces onto wooden skewers and place them in a shallow baking dish. Set aside.

Meanwhile mix orange juice, wine, onions, both jellies, honey, lemon juice, lime juice, and kumquats in a saucepan, heat until just about to boil. Season to taste. Pour half this mixture (reserving remaining mixture) over chicken skewers. Marinate for 2 hours.

While the chicken is marinating, prepare the rice. Boil a large pot of water and add the wild rice. Boil for 5 minutes then add the brown rice. Boil together for a further 10 minutes then add white rice and simmer for 15 minutes. Drain thoroughly and keep warm.

Heat a grill pan, barbecue, or broiler and cook the chicken skewers until cooked through, brushing them with the remaining kumquat mixture as they cook.

Fold the finely sliced fresh basil and chopped pistachio nuts through the rice. Serve with the chicken skewers. Drizzle with remaining kumquat mixture.

Desserts

Indian pistachio dumplings

Bring 300 ml (10 fl oz) of water to the boil in a pan and add the salt and the oil. Reduce the heat and add the rice flour, stirring constantly until a ball is formed. Remove from the heat and leave until cool enough to handle, then knead into a soft pliable dough.

To make a sugar syrup, heat the sugar and a dash of water until sugar has dissolved. Add the coconut and pistachios. Stir for 1 minute, then remove from the heat. Add the cardamom powder and 2 tablespoons of water and combine well.

Make small balls of the dough. Take a ball of dough in your palm and flatten it into a disc. Place a portion of the coconut mixture in the middle of the disc and fold up the edges to make a dumpling. Form the dumplings into large teardrop shapes.

Steam the dumplings for 20 minutes or until done. Serve drizzled with hot ghee.

SERVES 4

pinch salt

2 tbsp sunflower oil

225 g (8 oz) rice flour

150 g (5 oz) sugar

100 g (3½ oz) coconut, grated (shredded), if fresh, or desiccated (dry, unsweetened shredded)

100 g (3½ oz) unsalted pistachios, crushed finely

1 tsp ground cardamom

4 tbsp ghee, warmed

Desserts

Indian yoghurt banana cake

SERVES 6

3 oz/85 g desiccated (dry,
  unsweetened shredded) coconut,
  toasted

125 g (4½ oz) ghee or clarified
  butter

150 g (5 oz) caster (superfine) sugar

40 g (1½ oz) brown sugar

2 eggs

3 very ripe bananas

200 g (7 oz) Greek (strained plain)
  yoghurt

250 g (9 oz) self-raising (self-rising)
  flour

1 tsp cinnamon

½ tsp mixed spice (apple pie spice)

200 g (7 oz) sour cream or crème
  fraîche

100 g (3½ oz) (confectioner's) sugar

50 g (2 oz) toasted shredded
  coconut

Preheat the oven to 190°C/375°. Line the base of a 22–24 cm (8–10 in) non-stick springform tin (pan) with baking parchment. Grease the sides and pour in the toasted coconut. Tip the tin all around to coat the greased sides with the coconut, then pour out the excess and reserve for the cake batter.

Beat the ghee and sugars in a bowl until creamy, then add the eggs, one at a time, beating well after each addition.

Mash the bananas and add to the ghee/sugar mixture with the yoghurt, flour, cinnamon, spice and remaining coconut and stir to combine with a wooden spoon. Tip the mixture into the prepared tin and smooth the top.

Bake 55 minutes, or until firm and 'springy' when touched in the centre. Remove from the oven, allow to cool for 15 minutes, then remove the sides of the tin and cool completely. Remove the base and baking paper and place on a platter.

To make the icing, mix together the sour cream and icing sugar until thick and spreadable, then spread over the top of the cool cake. Pour the shredded coconut over the cream, until thickly covered.

Indian rice pudding with pistachios

Preheat the oven to 150°C/300°F. Place the rice, milk and evaporated milk in a heavy pan and bring to a simmer, taking care not to let the mixture boil. Simmer, uncovered, for 10 minutes.

Grease an ovenproof dish. Transfer the rice mixture to the dish, then stir in the cardamom seeds, cinnamon, sugar, almonds and pistachios, reserving 1 tablespoon to decorate. Bake for 2 hours, or until reduced to a thick consistency, stirring in the skin that forms on top every 30 minutes. Remove the cinnamon stick. Serve warm or cold, topped with the reserved pistachios.

SERVES 4

55 g (2 oz) basmati rice

450 ml (¾ pint) whole milk

400 g (14 oz) can evaporated milk

butter, for greasing

3 cardamom pods, husks discarded and seeds reserved

1 cinnamon stick

55 g (2 oz) caster (superfine) sugar

2 tbsp flaked (slivered) almonds, toasted

30 g (1 oz) shelled pistachios, roughly chopped

Desserts

Gulab jamun

SERVES 6

175 g (6 oz) sugar

8 green cardamom pods

30 g (1 oz) self-raising (self-rising)
*   flour*

125 g (4½ oz) powdered skimmed
*   milk*

30 g (1 oz) ghee or butter

30 g (1 oz) cream (farmer's) cheese

1–2 tbsp rosewater

2–3 tbsp milk or natural (plain)
*   low-fat yoghurt*

oil, for deep-frying

Put 150 g (5 oz) of the sugar with the 175 ml (6 fl oz) water in a wide pan or deep frying-pan. Stir over gentle heat until sugar has dissolved, then add cardamom pods. Increase heat and boil for 15 minutes to make a light syrup. Reduce heat to lowest setting to keep syrup warm.

Combine flour and powdered milk in a bowl. Rub in ghee or butter, then add remaining sugar, cream cheese, rosewater and enough milk or yoghurt to form a soft dough. Knead lightly and roll into 18 small balls.

Heat oil for deep-frying. Cook the dough balls in small batches, keeping them moving in the oil until they are golden brown all over. Remove with a slotted spoon and drain on kitchen paper for 5 minutes. Remove syrup from heat and add the cooked dough balls. Allow to cool to room temperature in syrup. To serve, transfer to individual plates with a slotted spoon, then add 2–3 tablespoons syrup.

Note: These small dumplings in a spicy syrup are a traditional dessert. They are usually made with full-fat powdered milk. This is not always easy to obtain, so this recipe uses skimmed milk powder and adds cream cheese.

Indian carrot cake

Preheat the oven to 180°C/350°F. Grease a large non-stick loaf tin (pan), then dust it lightly with some of the flour. Set aside.

In a large bowl, mix together the eggs, cardamom, mixed spice, ground cloves, sugar and ghee and whisk until the batter is smooth. Add the carrots, orange zest, nuts and sultanas, then add the flour, mixing to combine.

Pour the batter into the prepared tin and bake for 45 minutes, or until the top of the cake is golden brown and 'springy' when pressed gently in the centre. Remove the cake from the oven and allow to set for a few minutes, then turn out onto a wire rack to go cold.

Dust with icing sugar before serving.

SERVES 4

4 large eggs

1 tsp ground cardamom

1 tsp mixed spice (apple pie spice)

¼ tsp ground cloves

450 g (1 lb) sugar

100 g (3½ oz) ghee, softened, or vegetable oil, plus extra for greasing

200 g (7 oz) carrots, grated (shredded)

zest of 1 orange

55 g (2 oz) pistachio nuts, chopped and toasted

55 g (2 oz) cashew nuts, chopped and toasted

115 g (4 oz) sultanas (golden raisins)

230 g (8 oz) self-raising (self-rising) flour

icing (confectioner's) sugar, for dusting

Desserts

Recipe index

US: $19.99
UK: £16.99